SAD LITTLE MAN

Josh Overton

SAD LITTLE MAN

OBERON BOOKS
LONDON

WWW.OBERONBOOKS.COM

First published in 2017 by Oberon Books Ltd
521 Caledonian Road, London N7 9RH
Tel: +44 (0) 20 7607 3637 / Fax: +44 (0) 20 7607 3629
e-mail: info@oberonbooks.com
www.oberonbooks.com

A catalogue record for this book is available from the British
Library.

PB ISBN: 9781786822444
E ISBN: 9781786822451

FOREWORD

Any good Artistic Director spends a lot of time on trains.

A lot of my job involves travelling around the country looking for new work and new voices for the stage. It's taken me to a lot of new towns and cities, University studio theatres and converted rooms above pubs.

It's taken me to even more terrible guest houses, my 'favourites' including sleeping in a ninety-year-old woman's bed while she insisted on sleeping in the hallway outside, sharing a bunk-bed with a seventy-year-old man who'd recently been let out of prison and warned me he "screamed in his sleep", and sleeping in the foetal position in a single bed that'd been sawn to only five feet long to fit it into a tiny room.

And, despite all these endeavours, it is rare any Artistic Director finds something truly exciting on their travels. However, I will remember seeing Josh Overton's work, early in its development, for the rest of my life.

The first time I saw Josh and his company Pub Corner Poets perform was on one of my semi-regular visits to Hull. New Diorama have lots of links to the city and the University Drama department had set up a day of shows to see. I sat through them all and, while there were some interesting pieces, there was nothing to frantically text the office about.

At the end of the schedule, just as I was going to get my train back to London, I was told there was another group who wanted to see me. They'd been mostly performing their work in pubs and had set up in a small back-street night club, hoping we'd go along to see what they were working on. To this day I can't think of an offer that would be more irresistible to an AD than that.

The show was *ANGRY*. It went on to win the Sunday Times Playwright Award at National Student Drama Festival, having been booed and jeered on stage during its first performance, reminiscent of the audience rioting during the opening performance of Jarry's *Ubu Roi* back in 1896. The show went on to split audiences and critics at the Edinburgh Festival – being nominated for a coveted Total Theatre Award. And, finally, sold out performances at New Diorama in London.

Juvenile yet world-weary, *ANGRY* established Josh as a writer with a raw talent and craft. Meaning my second visit to Hull to see a first draft of Josh's work was taking place, not in a back street nightclub, but in a glossy, clean rehearsal room at Hull Truck Theatre.

But could lightning strike twice?

And it did. Even there in the Jerwood-ified, clean rehearsal room, Josh's new play completely transfixed the gathered audience of fellow artists and theatre staff – but this time not with anger but with a lyrical, porous sadness. Sat at the back of that room I watched as, within minutes, the small crowd were held by the piece as the meetings they'd just stepped out of and the mobiles in their pockets slowly drifted out of focus.

Having seen *Sad Little Man* now in a variety of forms, I find the gentler it is the deeper it cuts. Josh is at the beginning of his writing career. He will go on to write bigger plays, with growing ambition and audiences. But I can't imagine a more electric experience than sitting in that nightclub and rehearsal room hearing his words for the first time. In my career as an Artistic Director, nothing yet has come close.

David Byrne,
London 2017

Thanks

A big thank you must go to Tom Bellerby of Hull Truck Theatre and David Byrne of the New Diorama Theatre. Tom for giving us the opportunity to build *Sad Little Man* in the first place and Dave for letting us premiere it in his lovely theatre, both should also be given a great deal of credit for the time they've spent forcing me to be a proper playwright who does things with his life. They have both been very nice to me.

Thanks to the staff of Larkin's Bar, especially Moss, the mad bastard who has juggled so many rotas to let me have time to make my work that I'm surprised I still have a job, and Carter, whose cynical wit, sincere affection, and excitement for all things literature has made many a boring shift just another opportunity to bounce ideas around.

As always – Tyler, Joanna and team PCP have all my love and thanks for their patience, dedication, skill and desire to do all the boring stuff I don't want to do.

Thank you to Toby the scientist, Rosie the self-professed cuddle-whore and Ellie the sweet bundle of nice things that make the not nice things less not nice.

And Rob Salmon, thank you for trying to teach me how to not be shit, I think I might be getting there.

Sad Little Man was first performed by The Pub Corner Poets
at the New Diorama Theatre's *Hull UK City of Culture Showcase*
from the 2–4 of February 2017. Its original cast were:

Lee	Oliver Strong
Emily	Danielle Harris

Producer	Joanna Morley
Director	Tyler Mortimer
Production Manager	Joanna Morley
Projection/ Lighting Designer	Adam Hutton
Sound Designer	Mat Oliphant
Movement Director	Chris Yarnell
Stage Design	Emma Phimister
Construction	Andy Ross
Assistant Stage Manager	Helen Fitchitt

Characters

LEE

He hasn't slept and he speaks with his hands.
Vaguely smart clothes. Has an elastic band around his left wrist.

EMILY

Prettier than Lee and moves like liquid. She wears colour.

A stage

A bath

A mic

[As the audience enter LEE is seen standing near his microphone, he greets them half-heartedly, perhaps he is nervous. His clothes are damp.

The tap drips.

It won't stop raining. Sometimes it's louder or quieter but it's always there.

'SAD LITTLE MAN' is projected behind him.

Once the audience is seated he approaches the mic, taps it

Once

 Twice

  Three times.

He goes to tap it again but stops himself. The mic is apparently on.

His performance starts with a story.]

LEE: Um.

 1

  2

   3

    and

[MUSIC PLAYS and the projection switches to 'THE END'. Whatever music is chosen, it must be in 3,4. The words are performed to the beat but in as natural a way as is possible.]

 Stop me

  Stop me

   Stop me if you've heard this one before.

Somewhere
There's
        a hill,
Not a very big hill,
But a hill
In Italy or somewhere, I've still not decided
Maybe middle America, I I I don't really mind.
But there's a hill.
And sat at the top of this little hill is a little house,
All wood
And brick
Six windows, front and back doors, one bedroom.
There is always a bottle of wine and one of whisky waiting on
the kitchen counter for their respective owners to come home.

And sitting outside on the small porch is a gentle old woman
and a grumpy old bastard.
She sits in a rocking chair
He sits in an adult chair for normal people
and spread out in front of them is all
                                these
                                    fields.

I'm seeing maybe corn and wheat
So there's just that gold
Dirty gold just left and right of them.

They watch the sun set every single day.
Then they talk into the night.
Hide inside when the air sets the chill into their bones.

Every few days the grumpy old bastard stands from his chair
and prepares to head into town,
Buy the groceries and do important things.

Every few days the gentle old woman gently reminds him to
take care,
Wear his seat belt.

Every few days the grumpy old bastard cracks a smile on the
one side of his face and says;

"If I was always as careful as you wanted me to be,
I'd have died of boredom years ago."

One Kiss
Car Start
Off He Goes

She sits on the porch and watches his car exhausts mix with
the kick-up from the dirt road dust and disappear.

He takes his time in town,
talks at length with chatty shop people
but he's always home in time for sundown.

Hand in hand they send off the day
The air is warm,
they taste it in their mouths when they breathe
it tastes of corn and dust and care
it tastes of not having been sad for over half their lives.

They are still in love.

One day the grumpy old bastard stands from his chair and
prepares to head into town,
Buy the groceries, chat with those enthusiastic youths at the
shop who really get on his nerves.

That same day the gentle old woman gently reminds him to
take care,
Wear his seat belt.

And like every day the grumpy old bastard cracks a smile on
the one side of his face and says;

"If I was always as careful as you wanted me to be,
I'd have died of boredom years ago."

One Kiss
Car Start
Off He Goes

Some days he's late home barely reaching the porch and
packing away bags
as the sun's glow reaches the distant city skyline.

Today, he's later than that.
There's been no wind today so the gentle old woman can still
see the tracks he left as he drove away.
And She knows.
She knows.
She pours one glass of whisky and one of wine
Sits and drinks them separately.

Tipsy, with both drinks done
She reaches a hand across and holds the arm
of the adult chair for normal people
The sun is gone.

She knows there was nothing he could've said on his deathbed
that hadn't already been said every day that he saw her,
No regrets,
She sits and lets the chill of the air set into her bones
and neglects to go inside.

[After a moment, LEE cracks a confused, apologetic smile.]

I don't
I don't have a segue-way for that
I don't really know where it belongs in this you know?
It doesn't connect to anything
it doesn't fit.

[Projection returns to 'Sad Little Man']

It should, I m– I mean it does
fit
It's just
I'm not quite sure why it's *there*. Why it kept

swimming to the
surface.

You're gonna have to forgive me tonight.
I'm a little – um –

unfocussed.

My name is Lee by the way. I forgot to – um– you know
before.

I quite like my name.

This is stand-up tragedy, I call it that because I'm not

very funny.

I do observational tragedy for
example

Stop me if you've heard this one before
[The next section is run at speed.]
have you ever laid in bed laid in bed? lied in bed lane in bed
been **lying** in your bed on your back looking at the – ceiling –
I wanted to call it roof floor – in your bed on your back looking
at the ceiling have you ever felt the urge to just extend your hand
out in front of your face 'til it fills u**P** a **P**art of your field of vision
and do you ever just lock your arm in place focus your eyes on
your hand so your bedroom looks like a 2D painting stuck to the
back of it do it for me now,

*[He extends his hand out in front of him, as it passes the mic stand the lights
change, maybe the music increases in volume, as well as this EMILY's hand
snakes out of the bath, imitating his movements but up, rather than forward.]*

and does everything just kinda stop for a second *[wince]* a second
[wince] just a second *[wince]* three and a half seconds and you
realise you have that epiphany don't you fuck you you have that
thought fuck me you think, I'm SO brilliantly fucking important,
every minute of my time that pa**SS**eS un**S**pent i**S S**upr**E**mely
fucking m**EA**ningful and no one else in the world seems to realise
it. Why do I sleep you think. Why does anything I do matter?
Will the moment where I lie in bed and stare at the back of my
hand some day stop being the most worthwhile thing I have
ever done and be replaced by something of value. The fact that
I have recognised this is nihilism incarnate and makes me better
and smarter and more important than anyone except I can't stop
looking at the back of my hand and actually do something ten
years have passed and my arm hurts I don't know who I am and
any time I try to find something anything to make my cold and

impossibly brief time on this planet feel like energy well spent
only convinces me that no such activity exists. We are all weak
but I am the weakest of all of us,
*[He breaths out heavily and with speed, retracting his hand. As it
passes by the mic the lights and sound return to their previous setting
and EMILY's hand disappears.]* Stand-up tragedy. I like to think
it's not just my brain that makes those noises.

Sometimes when I'm here I'll think about dying. A lot
actually, in a zen kind of way, I – I – it doesn't mean you're
depressed if you do the same thing too.

Sorry, I I'm not judging I'm just
looking for someone who gets it.

Sorry, tonight isn't about that,
or me really,
it's about us.
By which I mean she and I not you and me sorry I I I don't
mean to be unclear this is all just
happening a little too quickly to
                                    process.
I want to be clear but we're forced to see all this through my
eyes so I'm afraid we may be wandering wherever my sad
little thoughts will take us.

Sorry, I will stop apologising at some point.
Not yet though.
[He clears his throat before launching into his poem.]

I,
Don't ever ever wanna die
to look at me
it might be hard to see
the youth that should be stretched across my best intentions
but I am only twenty-three,
If there is weight in my frame
and a sigh to the way that I speak
It is not because I have lived long enough to become truly tired

In fact this shoulder sag and sluggish speech has sat with me
for three
and a half
seconds
so far
When it hits four
I'll let you know

MUSIC

[LEE and THE GIRL are stood apart, shirtless with pyjama trousers on.
Projected onto their bodies is the text conversation that follows.
When each one receives a text their body lights up with the words
and a vibration noise is heard. They then trace or type their response
out onto their chest before sliding it across to be "caught" by the other, the process
then repeats. When their light isn't on they are in total darkness.

EMILY writes:	**LEE writes:**
What you thinking?	Not much
You're so deep.	I
	Am a genius
You	
Are a cunt.	
	U know what
	U know what
What?	Ur the only person I know that texts
	you instead of u
YOU boring cunt.	U soulless whore
I love you	I know sweetpea
I'm horny and alone.	Oh really?
Yes.	
	… Ahem?
Yes sir.	

(A brief pause as LEE fumbles with his "phone" and his pyjamas before a picture of the actor's penis appears on his chest. He pauses for a moment as if contemplating whether the image is flattering enough before sliding it across to EMILY. In the darkness we hear a giggle.)

Cold is it?

Nah, just ur mums not as pretty as she used to be

Oh my, that was almost a joke.

Beyr5ihffvbfsjbfwbfja fvj sfvjskblf

Wake up

I'm not asleep, I'm ignoring you.

U in bed?

On my way to the bath actually.

Exciting lives we lead.

Yes.

I saw Cheryl today.

We hear what sounds like rain taking over the sound of music, maybe in the dark we've convinced ourselves that we can see it. LEE is distracted moving the mic as if out of the rain to another part of the stage– silhouetted by two thunder claps, one blue, one red – as EMILY climbs into the bath and watches.]
[Lights change.]
[LEE reads from what looks like a diary – the words are unfamiliar to him, the music has stopped but it's trying to start again.]

LEE: 'I am unsure as to how we met. In my head it was in a park and it was raining but he remembers it differently and there was no third person there to confirm either version of events. I realise now that what should be an important memory for both of us isn't actually real in any tangible sense. I feel as though this should sadden me. Perhaps I'm too cold. But I know he wouldn't care either. The bags under his eyes were pretty and he forgot my name by the end of the conversation. That is what I would tell our kids, and it is how I remember it. Our kids probably would not care. Genetics are strong and they aren't real.

I suppose then that I'm writing this down for another reason.
[Gently the music begins to work again and the rain quietens.]
I'll have two children.
This is hypothetical so Lee's decisions don't matter. He's a flip
flopper on the baby issue anyway so we may not end up with any.
But in this version of my life I'll have two. Thank you very
much. Boy and girl, one smart and one happy, not fussed which
is which. They know me, as most kids do, much better than their
dad. If they're lucky and work lets him he starts and ends each
day with them and like all kids they won't realise the sacrifice
he's made for them 'til they're in their twenties.
One being inquisitive and the other being more of the
following type they ask me what their daddy is. *[not 'is like'
'is']* I say that their daddy is gentle, *[LEE begins to let slip his
emotions a little, for the moment it seems we are getting a true insight
into what EMILY thinks of him]* although he's more than twice
the size of you and can be a grumpy bastard there is no one
less scary in the world, I say that their daddy is very easily
confused sometimes and never means to be mean,
I say that their daddy is someone I will love to the day I die.

The smart one knows I'm lying.
I can see it in those beady little eyes they got from me.
I'm panicking
I say that their daddy is
Their daddy is
*[LEE realises that there are no more words and the rest of the pages are
blank he flicks through them until he reaches the final two pages.]*

Their daddy is making this up as he goes along
[Next page.]
I've never had a diary'
[LEE reacts.] Oh yeah.
[At speed the book is whipped out of LEE's hand by nothing.]
Shit. *[As a gut reaction towards losing something precious he dives
after it as it is pulled under the bath. Music snap off. The lights do
not change they should still be lighting a scene that LEE has stopped
taking part in although we can see him and what he's doing in the
space between this scene and the one about to start. He slides an arm
under the bath in an attempt to retrieve the diary, he grabs hold of*

27

something and pulls. It turns out to be a pair of high heels, angrily he throws them behind him and tries again. He grabs something and pulls. It turns out to be a trio of helium balloons, already tethered to the front of the bath they float into the air. He tries again, grabbing something heavier and pulling with all his strength. EMILY slides out from under the bath, she is now wearing make-up and carrying a handbag. Neither of them know it but the handbag is important.]

==========*[The lights and music completely change, the room is vibrant and colourful, briefly they stare at each other before the music kicks in and LEE lifts her off the floor, they dance as he carries her, carefully picking up each high heel with the appropriate foot, this can be (and perhaps it would be more human if it was) a clumsy process with giggling and failure, the next sequence can not.][As the music continues they, arm-in-arm, enter a "room" through a doorway, (perhaps a real frame that has slid on or an imagined one) with LEE covering EMILY's eyes. The room lights up and we hear pops as party streamers fall from the ceiling, perhaps we hear a "surprise" from an unseen crowd. They dance in circles, catching shot glasses tossed on from either side of the stage, shotting them and tossing them off the opposite sides before carrying on, kissing as a cute couple does before separating to meet the invisible guests. As LEE was covering EMILY's eyes we have established that this run of the motif is for her birthday, as such LEE's 'conversations' are in reference to her while hers are full of mimed 'thank yous' and the like. Criss-crossing the stage to greet members of the party they quickly meet up in the centre, animatedly chatting. Briefly their gestures become slow, exaggerated and violent. They are lit from their chests, similar to the phones but uglier and violent rain takes over the soundtrack. After a moment this all is immediately forgotten and the two pose for a photo. They turn and perform the sequence in reverse up stage with it being LEE's 'birthday' the movements are sloppier after each time they take a shot with conversations and kisses more grotesque, more desperate. As the two end up closer to the bath EMILY reaches out, for the balloons perhaps or the bath itself and LEE hauls her back in, the conversation is now tenser and heavier, the breaks for rain longer and harder, again the photo interrupts.][This dance can continue as many times as a director sees fit but they must always get drunker and fightier.]==========*

[The sequence ends with the characters breaking from their argument, EMILY drops her handbag and passes out, drunk or tired it doesn't matter, LEE picks her up as if to put her to bed then slings her over his shoulder before stretching his arm out past the microphone as he has done once before, the lights return to that state but we see very faintly the red and blue of before and the rain becomes distant and we hear a groaning, almost as if the roof is getting ready to collapse. LEE stares at the back of his hand.]

LEE: They'll be everywhere in the flat, On the taps

    I turned it on, wanted to wash

    All the –

    Made sure to

        you know

            twist it

    Off

    She doesn't like the dripping

    Pokes me in the

        ribs when I leave it on.

  –   It hurts

[As he says this we see a flash of metal in EMILY's hand. She wriggles free and wonders towards the bath tracing the air as she goes. The groan gets louder until –]
[All at once LEE pulls his hand back and the lights return to normal, the music gone and EMILY uses her knife to sever the strings of two of the balloons tied to the bath. LEE says:]
Sorry I –
[LEE is a little drunk.] [He clears his throat addressing the audience again.]
You – you forget the hits and count the misses I suppose. I do. But I still feel like we argue a lot. Over little things, minor money troubles or that miserable music shit she insists on playing on *my* speakers while I'm trying to sleep. We do fight. Because I'm special. Normal couples are safe and happy aren't they, but if you fight or convince yourself that what you have is fighting, with all the passion – bridled or un – then you're dark aren't you, and fire. You're life, You're actually living. She **knows you** like **no** ordinary woman could **know you**

and **you** have tamed the rage of something bigger and better
than anything **you know. You know.**
I know
knowknowknow
I know that
I know she's smarter than me.
Has more value
To society
In a eugenicsey sort of way.
You understand.
Shoot me in my sleep and a few lovely old people have to wait
longer for someone to pull their pint every sunday afternoon.
It's not,
not the same with her.
She matters.
And she'll matter more.
*[As he is saying this EMILY, holding a balloon in each hand, approaches
him from behind.]*
Doesn't mean she can't be super fucking wrong once in a while
*[Music, he grabs a balloon from her and she laughs in his face, as he
scream shout raps, she at normal speed performs a series of actions that
mimic one half of an argument.]*

[Music, heavy, bass-ey, something you'd want to shout to.]

Stop me if you've heard this one before
She is stubborn to a fault.
In that she is only stubborn in her attempts to avoid fault
This is not now nor has it ever been
the issue
the issue
is that I do not possess the energy willpower or capacity to pit
passion to passion for seven hours straight
Sometimes I will find myself at half past three pitching wits
with slick–shout–spit expertise worthy of winning a **war** but
find that breaking skull bone on brick wall would make the
stone bleed **more.**
I Will tell myself that this is normal
I Will tell myself that this is healthy

Maybe I will believe me,
But as hours of shouting turn to days of silence and thoughts turn
from talking to styles of violence I will know that I am lying.
So I must start telling truths again
*[He looks out to the audience and holds his hand out (lights again music
slows as does EMILY's actions).]*
[Utterly sincerely and more noticeably upset than he should be.]
I love you.
I'm so

      so sorry
Please Just say something, look at me.
I need it.
[Hand back, lights, music and EMILY back. As though nothing happened.]
Truths that make me feel weak to my soft little schoolboy
knees cuz Lee can't cut the conflict
But grovelling
turns to
talking
turns to
kissing

Kissing like a cute couple does
Kissing like only a cute couple can til one wrong step from
either **one** of us and **both** of us jump back on track like
fabricating fury is fun
So practised at acting our outrage out it's like fighting on fast
forward like –

*[LEE and EMILY by now have untied their balloons. Instantly they both
suck in as much helium as they can whilst leaving enough in there for
later. They argue at speed, as though someone has lent on the fast forward
button, their high pitched voices matched by the speed of their actions
(Note. EMILY's actions will be sped up versions of the ones she has been
doing up til now just with LEE filling in the other half).]*

EMILY: *Oh where have I heard*	**LEE:** *it's not like I won't*
That one before?	*Admit that it scares*
I know what you think	*the shit out of me*
But it's helping	*it does alright?*

33

It is   *I'm a scared pussy*
I know I've been a bit   *little bitch but I'm*
Off but I feel like I   *more scared for you*
Have a pretty fucking   *now than before. Yes,*
Good excuse don't you?   *You do and I'm being*
She knows what she's   *selfish but this is*
doing that's why I go   *our problem now you*
to her. You don't get   *made it our problem*
on I know but for fuck's   *And I'm fine with that*
sake Lee I need help we   *but you have to let my*
both *know that. Sometimes*   *opinion count for*
you just straight up   *something or why else*
refuse to see what I'm   *am I even here? Fuck*
trying to say I'm   *I am listening Jesus*
certain of that. Will   *of course I am this is*
you just shut the fuck   *really important shit*
up and accept that   *but it's not just gonna*
I'm happy, here,   *go away if we – fine fine*
with you? You cunt.   *FINE. You – yeah.*
I love you.

[Both defeated they let go of their balloons, the remaining helium blowing them away.]

[Then, something. They don't fight. Maybe they dance or fuck and forgive. Whatever happens they end up together on the floor. EMILY sleeps. LEE grabs the mic stand and lowers it gently down to his face.]

LEE: It makes certain that I'm sad sometimes, most things do I suppose.
God I'm –
[He laughs then makes a noise like the scream you do when you're dreaming.]

When I say sad I mean it in the way that kids do. Okay?
I I I I I really need you to get that. When grown ups say sad they don't mean that,
I mean –
When grown ups say
'HE is sad'

they mean
'HE is pathetic'
But I don't mean that.

I might be that but

I don't think I really get to to be the judge *of* that

[He leaves the mic against her chin and we hear her breath as he gets up and perches on the bath, it sounds like thunder.]

I leave her alone sometimes
Kinda feel like she deserves the whole bed to herself anyway.
I sit, on the edge of the bathtub and
I watch her through the door.
She looks like a 2D painting stuck to the back of my hand.
She looks safer from further away.

Sad.
SAD.

Kids you know –
they're the only ones who use words properly.
All this nuance and subtext and innuendo and social etiquette
and mismatched brain mouth message mumbo jumbo it
gets in the way. It messes with you're thinking, it wants you
to struggle to explain yourself so that the act of explaining
yourself is a reward unto itself. Eventually you get so wrapped
up in it you start to question if you even meant what you knew
you meant when you started this sentence.

[By now EMILY has risen, and returns to the bath with the mic. Handing it to him as he stands before disappearing into the water.]

There are too many words.
I have plans –

[Behind him EMILY turns the tap, finally silencing the drip we didn't know we could still hear.]
[With a real, almost psychotic violence to his voice, he seems like he might vomit.]
No not yet

Not yet
Please fucking just – Please –
I'm not –
No
No
    no
         NO
      no
no
Oi!
No
Fucking – Just –

EM–! *[She turns the tap back on, the drips all too real again.]*
Thank you Thank you I love you Thank you

I had
When I was a kid I had plans
I had
My dad
I I I would wait on the stairs for him every night
and he'd come home all tired from working at whatever it was
he did
but he'd never be grumpy
he'd say
"How are you – "
I remember this really
really well
he'd say
"How are you today little man?"
a – a – and I'd just straight up tell him the truth.

Isn't that so fucked up?
You ever think about
when was the last time you were just totally honest about
                            how you were feeling?
When was –
How old were you when doing that started to make you too
vulnerable

'Show don't tell' I suppose
but I don't think I have much show left in me

[Her arms snake out of the dark and hold him, one hand undoing shirt buttons.]

I need to sleep I think

Ah
  ha
   ah
Right
   ah
     fuck
   Let's
Let's
Ah
Fuck
Let's make this easier on all of us

Please
    for me
'Cause I'm gonna keep losing track of things
[And Breath and –]
I
  know
     where
       I am now.
Sorry.
I know where we are now.

[Music plays.]

Uh,

The fuck is this miserable shit?

No
No hang the fuck on
Not yet

I'm not –

OI

[Off mic he addresses an uncaring tech box.]

Can we just – ?
Look
please?

Okay.
[Beat.]
[Back on mic.] TURN THE FUCKING MUSIC OFF
I CAN'T FU- *[It goes.]*-cking
think.
[Beat.]
I can't.

Okay, um.
Let us make this easy for all of us here.
Cuz I know there ain't no way to speak how I think without
sounding like I'm trying to say more than I am.
So Imma speak with kid language.
Imma just Say words the way they were meant to be Said and
See if it meanS what I'm Saying.

[He bites the inside of his cheek.]
[He clicks his jaw.]

I am a sad little man
there's too much happening in my brain.
I'm sorry I'm the only one here who doesn't know what's going on.
I'm sorry I'm not as clever as you.
I would like this to stop please.
I –
[He looks down.]
Where's m –
shirt.
[He looks around briefly, EMILY has disappeared, his shirt with her.]

Where
Whrer

Whar

[Beat.]

[Confused and breathing heavily he leaves his spotlight, which attempts to follow him. As he crosses the stage he comes across another microphone, set as if he had been stood there and performing the whole time, EMILY, somewhere in amongst the bathtub, watches. Perhaps she is waiting for him to get it.] [LEE, more confused, approaches the mic.]

Stop me

LEE'S V/O: If you've heard this one before.

LEE: No

LEE'S V/O: knowknow

> I know that
> I know she's smarter than me.

[LEE leaves this spot in an attempt to find the previous one, instead he finds the old mic replaced with the hand bag, its contents spilled somewhat into the space and his shirt, damp. He finds her phone, the light of its home screen bringing his face out in the dark. The ceiling groan has returned. He types slowly but firmly onto the phone for a moment, then waits. His chest lights up with a message symbol and a name: 'EMILY'. He doesn't open it. At the same time as his chest gives off the ring tone:]

LEE'S V/O: I hope it's not just my brain that makes these noises

[His chest flashes and rings, he has texted himself again (Number on his chest going up)]

LEE'S V/O: Fuck you you have that thought fuck me you think

[Chest flash tone and number increase again. He looks down phone in hand at the number 3 on his chest. He is ready to text again but uncertain.] [Then:]

LEE'S V/O: In fact this shoulder sag and sluggish speech has sat with me for three
and a half
seconds
so far

[LEE waits trying to anticipate the next voice over, maybe moving or making noise in an attempt to activate it, until from the bath:]

EMILY: What happens when it hits four?

[LEE stops and turns, realising that this is the first time we've heard her speak not distorted in any way. He tries to speak but nothing comes out, until his voice over does it for him.]

LEE'S V/O: If I was always as careful as you wanted me to be I'd have –

[LEE kills the sound by texting again as he does so the screen on his chest warping and refusing to turn into the number 4 the stage and tech groans with the effort of it before shorting out. "EMILY 3 ½ messages". Sparks. LEE drops her phone which ends up kicked to a corner. As this happens EMILY cuts the string of the final balloon attached to the bath, strips down and climbs in, taking the knife with her. Workers lights come on. We are left with LEE on stage in full light. He moves about the space, really seeing it and us for the first time. He approaches the mic, he is much more awake now than he has been up to this point.]

LEE: um

[He realises the microphone isn't on, pauses, decides that it is on and speaks into it.]

    1

    2

    3

    4

[He decides the lights work again.]
[He decides that music is playing. The song that plays is the one from the opening. The song belonged to her. His speech is muddled by tears and misremembering the words.]

Stop me.

Somewhere there's a hill
I don't mind –

            – it doesn't matter where.
But on this hill there's this house right?

And I never cared what kinda house it was, what it looked like
as long as it's there.
And there is always a bottle of wine and one of whisky waiting
on the kitchen counter for their respective owners to come home.
Sitting outside on the small porch is a a grumpy old bastard

That one's meana be me.

And a gentle old woman.

Tha's

    tha's this one

He sits in an adult chair for normal people
And she sits in whatever stupid fucking chair she wants
and spread out in front of them is all

                      these

                          fields.

Gold.

LEE'S V/O: Stop me –

LEE: They watch the sun set Every Single day.
Then they talk into the night.
Hide inside when the air sets the chill into their bones.

Every few days the grumpy old bastard stands from his chair
and prepares to head into town,

Every few days the gentle old woman gently reminds him to
take care,
Wear his seat belt.

Every few days the grumpy old bastard cracks a smile on the
one side of his face and says;

"If I was always as careful as you wanted me to be,
I'd have died of boredom years ago."

One Kiss
Car Start
Off He Goes

She sits on the porch and watches his car exhausts mix with
the kick-up from the dirt road dust and disappear.

Wherever they are The air is warm,
they taste it in their mouths when they breathe
it tastes of corn and dust and care
it tastes of not having been sad for over half their lives.

They are still in love.

LEE'S V/O: Stop me –

LEE: But today he doesn't get to drive back

And She knows.
She fucking knows.
She pours one glass of whisky and one of wine
Sits and drinks them separately

Tipsy, with both drinks done
She reaches a hand across and holds the arm
of the adult chair for norm –

LEE'S V/O: Stop me.

LEE: She. Holds. The arm. Of. The. Adult chair for normal
people.

My fucking chair.

The sun is gone

[The music doesn't stop.]

I guess it fits in here

See that
That is how it's supposed to happen.
Then and only then is it okay to die.
You leave a happy fucking footprint alright?
You
you just do.
You
[He fiddles with the elastic band around his wrist for too long.]
You don't get words

45

You don't get to pretty it up
make it mean anything.

You just don't don't get don't get to say how you feel about it
'*I* don't' I Mean
'*I* don't'.
I have to get this right,
You?
You just get to stop.
You just get to stop right now.
And I get it
I get it cuz I've gotta keep moving
Planets revolving however many fucking miles a minute
The place where you stopped moving that's way off in space now
And my feet may be glued to the floor
but I am still fucking spinning away aren't I
spinning on a giant ball of cunts who aren't you.
Who won't ever become you
And I will never get to understand why that is.
I can only guess
I can *only* guess,
And I THINK it's because you're smarter than the rest of us.

I thought I might be as smart as you
cuz I'm not good at words
And I'm no fucking good at people
but I was sure I was good at you.

I was so sure

an'
I would forgive you
I would forgive you in a fucking second
Just
come back
Please

[Off mic, we cannot hear him say, 'I know there's no point asking,
                                        but,
                                                just in case.'

]

[Quietly into the mic.]

Fuck it.
Just let me sleep.

[He lies down in the wet and the blood. Taking the mic with him.
The dripping has stopped. He holds his hand above his head.]

I sometimes think of the ceiling as the **roof floor**. I like how the
letters of each word are so similar. Structure is safety.
[He waits for the show to end.]
[It doesn't.]
[He sighs.]
[He waits for the show to end.]
[It doesn't.]

It never ends you know? Each time you think you've got it, you
understand it, it just keeps going, you don't get a proper finish.
You haven't suffered enough or thought about it enough or
begged it to stop enough, I don't
I don't know.
I can't know can I?
I can't know can I?

[He jumps up.]
This is a private moment you are privy to.
You see here a man
Face in front of microphone
Trying to explain something he doesn't understand.
In poetry…
Because this is performance,
this is escapism
this is drown your worries in someone else's
But this is not Broadway
this is not day-time T.V.
this may be a made up man's mind
Cuz this right here and now
Will never be
Good enough,
I will never explain this well enough
and you will just have to let me keep on going

until I forget all the words
cuz this is stand-up fucking tragedy
Stop me if you've heard th –

[The music is interrupted by a phone call, EMILY's phone horribly vibrating against the floor and shining a small light out.]

[LEE makes noise.]
[He sinks and crawls to the phone and answers the call before collapsing back. EMILY's voice plays through the speakers, distorted by voicemail. She sounds calm.]

EMILY V/O: Lee. I know you're working so I texted a load but I guess I just wanna be certain you get the message. Uh. Could you come straight home when you're done if you can? I need you here.

I bought whisky.

Oh
I Love You.
A lot.

[The show stops holding its breath: the projection reads 'EMILY: 4 Messages' and music kicks in the same 'miserable shit' music from earlier. LEE scrambles to his feet and finally sees her for the first time for real, she floats in the bath, the water red.]

LEE V/O: 1
    2
       3
         and

[LEE runs, he attempts to lift her out of the water making non-stop noise. The music and the rain getting far too loud, eventually drowning out the noise, he drags her weight from the bath desperately looking for signs of life. He pushes on her chest and tries half CPR half terrified kissing. He ties the hair out of her face with his elastic band he cleans her with his shirt. LEE sees her, this is the last time she will be beautiful. Soon, maybe too soon, he gives up and slump sits against the bath. He cries without moving his face, then he stands, makes sure that tap has stopped dripping and climbs into the bath. He reaches for the roof floor. Then, he stops.]

[The music ends.]

[EMILY stands and makes her way to the mic.]

EMILY: Stop me if you've heard this one before.

I –

[Blackout. The rain ends.

The End.]

Printed in the USA
CPSIA information can be obtained
at www.ICGtesting.com
LVHW020945171024
794056LV00003B/984